nitty gritty books

Pasta & Rice	Crepes & Omelets	To My Daughter, With Love
Calorie Watchers Cookbook	Microwave Cooking	Natural Foods
Pies & Cakes	Vegetable Cookbook	Chinese Vegetarian
Yogurt	Kid's Arts and Crafts	The Jewish Cookbook
The Ground Beef Cookbook	Bread Baking	Working Couples
Cocktails & Hors d'Oeuvres	The Crockery Pot Cookbook	Mexican
Casseroles & Salads	Kid's Garden Book	Sunday Breakfast
Kid's Party Book	Classic Greek Cooking	Fisherman's Wharf Cookbook
Pressure Cooking	Low Carbohydrate Cookbook	Charcoal Cookbook
Food Processor Cookbook	Kid's Cookbook	Ice Cream Cookbook
Peanuts & Popcorn	Italian	Blender Cookbook
Kid's Pets Book	Cheese Guide & Cookbook	The Wok, a Chinese Cookbook
Make It Ahead French Cooking	Miller's German	Japanese Country
Soups & Stews	Quiche & Souffle	Fondue Cookbook

designed with giving in mind

Dearest Daughter:

  Here is the cookbook you asked for. I have designed it around our favorite family menus, as you requested.

  I am sure that it will help you to have successful dinner partie with confidence and which you, yourself, will enjoy.

  You may remember family dishes you don't find here. Let me know about them and when next we are together we can add them.

       Love,
      Mother

To My Daughter, With Love

...A collection of family recipes.

by Wanda Groceman

Illustrated by Mike Nelson

Table of Contents

Menus

As you know, most of our national holidays have always been family feast days --- times for family and friends and good food prepared from favorite family recipes, proudly served and fondly remembered.

Birthdays in the family have also involved special dinners, and it is our tradition that the guest of honor chooses both the menu and the cake to be served.

Christmas or Thanksgiving
Dinner for 12 or more (usually more)

Ambrosia

Relish Tray: celery sticks, green and ripe olives, sweet pickles, spiced peaches, watermelon preserves

Cranberry Sauce

Roast Turkey   Giblet Gravy

Mashed Potatoes   Candied Yams

Bacon Style Green Beans

Corn Pudding   Hot Rolls

Pumpkin Pie   Coffee   Fruitcake

At Christmas we always cut the fruitcake that had been mellowing in Brandy since early in November. Make it well before Thanksgiving and store it in a lovely tin, but don't forget it. Check it often to be sure it is moist with Brandy.

3

Favorite Fruitcake

1 lb. pecans, broken
3 ½ cups flour
½ lb. English
   walnuts, broken
✦ 1 cup butter
½ lb. red candied cherries
2 ¼ cups sugar
¼ lb green candied
   cherries
1 lb mixed candied fruit
8 ozs candied pineapple

2/3 cup margarine
2/3 cup milk
4 ozs. golden raisins
1/3 cup Brandy
6 eggs, separated
1/8 cup Rum
1 teaspoon cream
   of tartar
1 teaspoon pure vanilla
1 cup flour for the
   fruit and nuts

Grease, line with brown paper and grease again, 3 loaf pans and 1 angel cake tube pan. In a large roasting pan mix the candied fruit and nuts with the 1 cup flour. Set aside.

Cream the sugar, butter, and margarine. Add the egg yolks and beat at medium speed until quite creamy. Add the flour alternately with the liquids and the vanilla. Beat the egg whites with the cream of tartar until very stiff. Mix the cream mixture with the fruit and nuts. Fold in the egg whites gently but thoroughly. Fill the prepared pans about 2/3's full, dividing the batter equally. If you wish, two tube pans may be used. I use the three small loaf pans because these cakes make such nice gifts. Bake at 275° for about 3 hours. Cool on a rack in the pans. When cool, remove from pans and drizzle 1/4 cup of Brandy over them. Store in tightly sealed containers but check on them once a week. If all the Brandy appears to be absorbed add another 1/4 cup of Brandy in the same manner.

Cranberry Sauce

For twelve persons you will need to make two recipes of Cranberry Sauce. Don't try to double the recipe - it is much better to use two different pots than try to make it all in one.

8

1 lb. fresh Cranberries washed and picked over for stems.
1 cup water

Cook in a 4 quart saucepan with the lid on for about 10 minutes (after it boils). Add 2 cups of sugar and stir until all sugar is dissolved. Cook with the lid off for about 5 minutes over a low flame. Remove from heat and pour into a bowl. Cool to room temperature. Refrigerate. This keeps well so make it several days ahead.

The day before the feast: cook the turkey giblets in 2 or 3 quarts of water. When they are almost tender add salt to taste and add a little more water if it has boiled away. Remove the giblets and, chopping only the amount needed for the gravy, store separately in very well sealed containers in the refrigerator. Save the broth for the dressing.

Make cornbread and biscuits and set aside for the dressing.

Cornbread

2 eggs
2 cups buttermilk
2 cups cornmeal
3 teaspoons baking powder
1 teaspoon baking soda

1½ teaspoons salt
1½ cups flour
1 Tablespoon sugar
4 Tablespoons hot oil
or bacon fat

Beat eggs and milk together. Sift the dry ingredients and add the egg-milk mixture. Heat a 9"x 13"x 2" pan with the 4 Tablespoons fat in it. Coat the pan well with the fat. Pour off the remaining fat into the bread mixture and beat well. Fill the oiled pan and bake at 400° for about 35 to 40 minutes. Cut into squares and set aside for dressing.

Biscuits

12

3 cups flour
1 teaspoon salt
4 teaspoons baking powder

1 teaspoon soda
½ cup shortening
1½ cups buttermilk

Sift the dry ingredients together and cut in the shortening. Add the milk and mix with a large spoon. Turn out onto a floured board or pastry cloth. Knead some of the flour into the dough. When the dough is no longer sticky, roll or pat out to about ½" thickness. Cut with a biscuit cutter and place on a well-greased baking sheet that has already been heated. Bake at 450° for 12 minutes or until golden brown. Set aside for dressing.

13

Corn Pudding

1 can white cream style corn
1 #2 can whole yellow corn
2 eggs, separated
1 Tablespoon sugar
14 ½ cup evaporated milk
3 Tablespoons butter

2 Tablespoons
  chopped onion
⅛ teaspoon pepper
nutmeg
paprika
½ teaspoon salt

    Beat egg yolks and milk. Add corn, seasonings, and melted butter. Beat egg whites stiff but not dry. Fold into corn mixture. Pour into baking dish from which it can be served at the table. Now the pudding is ready for the oven. Refrigerate until the day of the feast. On that day remove pudding from refrigerator and bake about 45 minutes. If pudding does not brown well at 350°, sprinkle the top with a little more nutmeg and place it under the broiler - but don't burn.

15

This casserole will serve 6 with ease. Make two of these for 12. If you have too many "oven-dishes" this casserole may be baked a little early and then reheated at serving time but it will not look as nice.

Ambrosia

6 oranges
2 Delicious apples
2 cups sugar
1½ cups pineapple chunks
1 cup coconut (moist flakes)
1 cup broken walnut meats

16

    Cut away the peeling on the oranges. Cut into bite size chunks. Peel, core, and chop the apples. Quickly toss all the ingredients together.
    Store in the refrigerator in a covered

container for at least 24 hours - longer if you like.

Do not make a substitution for the walnuts. this recipe gets its flavor from these nuts. I like serving this at the table from my prettiest compote dish.

Put the celery hearts and sticks in a bag and refrigerate. Chop enough celery to make 2 cups. Chop very fine 1½ cups onion. Seal these in a refrigerator dish until you make the dressing.

Candied Yams

Use the large size can of yams (1 lb. 12 ozs. I believe).

Drain the liquid into a saucepan and add the juice from one can of apricots (a #2 can). Heat over a medium flame and add 1 cup brown sugar and 4 Tablespoons butter. Cook until thick. Meanwhile arrange the yams and apricot halves in a baking dish. Pour the syrup over the yams and dot with more butter. Refrigerate until feast day. On that day bake about 45 minutes at 350°. The last 15 minutes add marshmallow bits to the casserole if you happen to like marshmallows. If not - sprinkle the top generously with cinnamon and sugar as I do.

A Word About Pies

I think a good pumpkin pie is better than the mock mince of the commercial variety - although that can be great with a little help - Brandy sauce etc.

If the dinner hour is to be early in the afternoon you may bake your pies the evening before, however the custard base pies look and taste better if served the same day they are baked. I like dinner around 5 p.m. which allows ample time in the morning for making pies.

Pumpkin Pie

1½ cups canned pumpkin
½ teaspoon cinnamon
1½ cups evaporated milk
nut meg
3 eggs
1 cup sugar
dash salt
2 teaspoons butter
1 10" pie shell - unbaked

22

Beat eggs and milk, add pumpkin. Mix sugar and cinnamon. Add salt and pumpkin mixture. Beat well with electric mixer. Pour into shell, dot with butter and sprinkle top lightly with nutmeg. Bake at 425° for about 30 minutes. 23 A stainless knife blade carefully inserted in the center of the pie will come out clean if the pie is done. Serve with whipped cream. A pie of this size should serve 8 persons. Make two pies for 12 servings.

Holiday arrives: Early in the morning I finish the dressing, using the biscuits and cornbread from pages 11 and 12.

Cornbread dressing

Remove the 2 cups celery and 1½ cups chopped onion from refrigerator. Melt ½ cup of butter in a large fry pan and add the celery and onion. Sauté on medium heat for 10 to 15 minutes. Meanwhile break the biscuits and crumble the cornbread into a very large pan. Add the sauteed celery and onion to this. Heat the reserved giblet broth and add, a cup at a time, to the bread. Now beat in 2 teaspoons salt, ½ teaspoon black pepper and 1 Tablespoon sage (ground). The mixture should be rather fluid at this point, rather like a thick pudding. With a large spoon beat in 5 large or 6 medium eggs. Taste for salt and seasonings. Stuff the neck and cavity and put the remaining dressing in a baking pan. The extra pan may be baked later for 1 hour at 350°. During that time baste the dressing a few times with pan drippings from the turkey. This is a nicely browned dressing and may be served instead of the stuffing in the bird.

26

Cooking the Bird

A 16 to 20 lb. hen turkey should serve 12 nicely. Since cooking time varies with each bird, follow the chart on the wrapper, allowing 1 hour more. This will give a time for further cooking if needed, and a period for the bird to "Rest" before you begin carving.

If you have only one oven it may be necessary to bake the bird well in advance of the dinner hour so that the extra casseroles will have the last hour in the oven. In that event do not reheat the turkey, but slice it, and depend on your gravy to heat it at the table.

Cover the entire bird with a tent of aluminum foil. Remove it to baste every half hour or so, and remove it entirely near the end of the cooking time if additional browning is needed.

Put one or more of your guests to work making up the relish tray, and refrigerate it until serving time.

The Table

The table is something else you may want help with, especially if you must use it for the holiday breakfast first. So, set it up as early as possible. Then, in the last hour, use your helpers to set out the cranberry sauce, the ambrosia in little sauce dishes for each place, the relish tray, ice and water in the tumblers, and any other of the traditional additions that are peculiar to your family.

Make the giblet gravy, cover and set on a keep-warm burner.

Giblet Gravy

3 cups broth and a cup of drippings from the turkey
6 tablespoons cornstarch mixed with enough cold water to make a thin paste
½ cup chopped giblets
1 chopped hard-boiled egg
salt and pepper to taste

Bring the reserved giblet broth to a boil, add the cup of pan drippings to this. Lower the heat and stir in the thin cornstarch paste. Cook and stir until the gravy boils and becomes clear. Add the giblets and egg and cover. Keep on heat, but do not boil, until serving time.

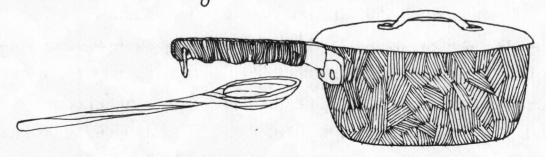

Potatoes

For your mashed potatoes boil them in salted water only until they are fork-tender. Add heated cream and plenty of butter as you whip them in your electric beater. Salt and pepper to taste and be sure to have your covered serving dish hot.

The last 15 minutes before dinner heat your favorite rolls. Whip the cream for the pie. If you wish to be safe as far as the cream holding up, add 1/4 teaspoon cream of tartar to 1 pt. whipping cream. When soft peaks form, add 3 Tablespoons sugar and

3*

1 teaspoon vanilla, beat until stiff, and refrigerate until dessert time.

Before you leave the kitchen be sure the coffee is plugged in, and there you have the feast.

From these pages make a list and a time-table and add any other things that require preparation. Then, as you work, check off the list to be sure everything comes along on schedule. Happy Holiday!

Our New Years Eve Late Supper

Marinated Herring   Smoked Oysters
   Hot Crab Dip with Wheat Thins
Pickled Pigs Feet   Butter
   Barbecue Brisket of Beef Western
         Broccoli Casserole
Rice Vert Pudding   or Baked Potato
   Tossed Salad - Blue Cheese Dressing
              and / or
   Grandma's Green Cabbage Cole Slaw
         Strong Black Coffee
Favorite Fruitcake Candy and Nuts

Late Supper

At New Year's or any time! Check your market for the herring, oysters, and any other extras you wish to add.

Well in advance of the party, marinate and bake the brisket.

Barbecue Brisket of Beef Western

A 6 lb. flat cut of brisket (fresh, not corned) serves 8 to 10. Wash it and season both sides with a mixture of these:

½ teaspoon garlic salt   ¼ teaspoon ground coriander
½ teaspoon celery salt   ½ teaspoon onion powder

If you have a barbecue, cook the brisket on it over even coals.

On the other hand, if you are going to use your oven, do it this way:

Place the meat in a glass pan and pour 3 ozs of liquid smoke over all. Seal tightly with plastic wrap and refrigerate at least 24 hours.

Starting with a cold oven with the temperature

control set for 275°, bake in a uncovered roasting pan in the marinade for about 4 hours - perhaps longer. When meat is fork-tender remove from oven. Briskets vary a great deal so, if moisture disappears from the pan during baking, add enough water to cover the bottom of the pan.

When the meat is cool it can then be refrigerated or frozen. If it is only a day or two until your party then just seal the brisket and refrigerate. The "day of": Slice the meat very thin and replace it in a shallow baking pan 9"x 13"x2".

Barbecue Sauce

1 cup prepared Barbecue Sauce
½ cup water
½ cup brown sugar
1½ cups ketchup
½ teaspoon salt

42

Cook all together on medium heat for 15 to 20 minutes. When the sauce has cooked down enough it will take on a rather dark color and should be removed from the heat until time to heat the meat once more.

This sauce may be served separately or a small amount may be poured down the center of the sliced brisket before it is reheated in a moderate oven. Do not heat for a long period as this will only dry out the meat.

43

A few times I have been unfortunate in getting brisket that was quite fat. Should this happen to you (God forbid) be sure to trim off the fat as you slice the meat.

A baked potato is my preference with brisket, but for a crowd, green rice pudding is excellent. Make two recipes of this dish if you are serving more than 10 people.

44

Rice Vert Pudding

3 eggs
1 large can evaporated milk
4½ cups cooked rice
2/3 cup salad oil
3 small garlic cloves, finely minced
2 cups fresh parsley, finely minced
½ cup finely chopped onion
1½ teaspoons salt
½ teaspoon white pepper
1 teaspoon Lowrey's seasoned salt
½ cup heavy cream

46

8 oz package velveeta cheese
paprika

Beat the milk, eggs, and salad oil together in a large bowl. Add all the remaining ingredients except the cream and paprika. Mix well. Add the cream, mix, and pour into a 9" x 13" x 2" baking dish. Sprinkle the top lightly with paprika. Bake in a slow oven - 300° for about 1 hour or until set.

The broccoli casserole in the menu is so easy that it is simple to mix the "day of" and bake the last 20 minutes with the rice pudding.

Broccoli Casserole

2 bunches of broccoli
1 package onion soup mix
1 4oz. can mushrooms (stems and pieces)
1 cup heavy cream   seasoned bread crumbs
½ cup grated cheese (mild cheddar)

Cook the broccoli. Drain it and arrange in a long shallow baking dish with the stems all turned to the center.

Pour cream into saucepan. Bring to boil over medium heat. Stir in soup mix, cheese, mushrooms and their liquid.

Pour mixture down the center of the casserole, covering broccoli stems. Top with bread crumbs and dot with butter. Bake about 20 minutes at 350°. Serves 8 to 10.

Grandma's Cole Slaw

8 cups of shredded cabbage (get green cabbage if you can)
1 cup of finely chopped onion
1 cup chopped celery
½ cup vinegar
1 cup mayonnaise
juice of ½ lemon
½ cup sugar
¼ cup cream
salt and pepper

50

Wash and shred the cabbage early in the day.

Refrigerate this well-covered. Have the celery and onion ready in a separate covered container. Two hours before serving, toss the cabbage with celery and onion. Mix the vinegar, lemon juice and sugar. Add mayonnaise and cream. Pour over cabbage. Mix. Refrigerate until serving time.

51

Here is my tossed salad - great with this or any beef dinner.

Tossed Salad

52

1 head iceberg lettuce
1 head Boston lettuce
1 large cucumber, scored and thinly sliced)
4 green onions, chopped
8 radishes, sliced thin
1 cup celery, coarsely chopped

1 carrot, grated
6 large ripe tomatoes - quartered

Toss everything in a large salad bowl, reserving only the tomatoes. Refrigerate. Just at serving time toss with your favorite dressing and top with the tomatoes. Serves 8 to 10.

Favorite Blue Cheese Dressing

Blend together in your blender at low speed:

1 cup Miracle Whip salad dressing
1 cup buttermilk
54   1 teaspoon garlic salt
1 Tablespoon Worcestershire sauce
4 ozs blue cheese

Pour into refrigerator jar and add 4 ozs more crumbled blue cheese. Shake.

Tom's Birthday Menu

Crab Imperial
Pan grilled Delmonico Steak / with
Mushrooms
Baked Potato with Sour Cream
and Chives
Buttered Tiny Le Seur Peas
Head Lettuce / French Dressing
Double Chocolate Cake with
Vanilla Ice Cream

56

Since the January weather discourages outdoor grilling I have a pan-broil idea for you. Tom thinks this steak is quite as delicious as the charcoal grilled. We begin with the Crab Imperial:

Crab Imperial

2 small cans crab,
    drained and boned
½ teaspoon dry mustard
2 Tablespoons butter

½ cup red pepper, chopped
1 cup heavy cream
½ cup green pepper,
    chopped

1 Tablespoon Worcestershire sauce
1 teaspoon vinegar
salt and pepper
paprika
58 1½ cups seasoned bread crumbs

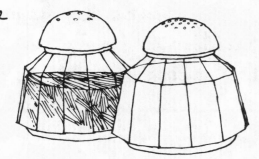

Heat cream, butter, and seasonings; add bread crumbs reserving ½ cup. Mix well. Add peppers and crab. Fill oyster shells (this will fill 24 small shells generously). Freeze here if desired. When ready to bake, top with the remaining crumbs, sprinkle with a little paprika and bake at 350° until brown and bubbly - about 20 minutes.

Baked Potatoes

When I bake potatoes I scrub them very clean, oil the skins, and prick them with a fork and bake in a slow oven without foil.

If you happen to go to Kansas City, get Wolferman's thousand Island Dressing - this is the best with head lettuce. French is also very good.

If you are not on a diet (we usually are) have garlic french bread toast with this.

Have all things ready when you start the steak. The table complete and the plates (preferably chop plates) hot.

Sauté ½ lb. fresh mushrooms - sliced - in a small amount of butter. This will require about 5 or 6 minutes. Stir continuously. Set aside to add at serving time. Have ready one medium sized antique-variety flatiron or other very heavy object.

Delmonico Steaks - Pan grilled with mushrooms

Have your butcher cut 4 steaks 1" thick and trim well. Get an extra piece of suet. Heat two cast iron skillets very hot and rub them well with suet. Two steaks should fit into each pan. Move the iron from one steak to the other (unless you just happen to have 4 irons lying around). Cook 5 minutes. Turn the steaks and cook another 5 minutes. Remove from pan to a hot platter. Pour ½ cup water in each pan — boil up the juices and salt well. Pour over the steaks on individual plates, add the mushrooms (on the side) and the baked potato.

Rush to the table! Have your salt and pepper mills handy for those who like more seasonings. Meanwhile the tiny La Seur Peas of the frozen variety are ready and should be served in a little sauce dish - on the side.

Double Chocolate Cake

1½ cups sugar
3 squares unsweetened
   chocolate
½ cup boiling water
64 ½ cup butter
2 teaspoons vanilla

2 eggs, well beaten
1 teaspoon soda
½ teaspoon salt
1 cup buttermilk
2 cups flour

Melt the chocolate in a small saucepan. Add the water and half the sugar. Cook and stir the mixture 'til smooth and glossy. Cool. Cream remaining sugar and butter until light and fluffy. Add the eggs and beat well. Add the cool chocolate mixture.

Sift the remaining dry ingredients together and add these alternately with the buttermilk. Beat well after each addition. Add vanilla. Pour into two greased and floured 9" layer cake pans. Bake for about 30 minutes at 350°. Turn onto cake racks and cool. Ice with fudge frosting.

Fudge Frosting

½ cup cocoa
1½ cups evaporated milk
3 cups sugar
dash of salt
66 2 teaspoons vanilla
2 Tablespoons light corn syrup
4 Tablespoons butter

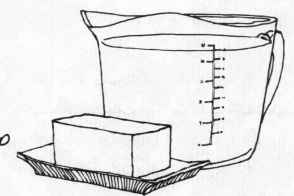

Mix cocoa and sugar in saucepan. Gradually add the milk and then the syrup and salt. Cook over medium heat to the soft ball stage. Remove from fire and add vanilla and butter. Cool slightly and beat until it is the right spreading consistency. If it seems too thick add a bit of cream.

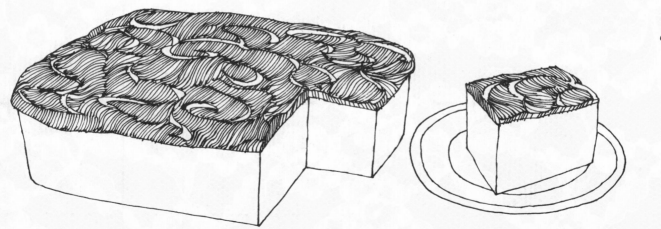

Papa's Birthday
February 7th

Ambrosia

Seafood Gumbo — Rice

Papa's Salad

Celery Sticks - Carrot Curls - little
sweet and hot peppers

Butter   Coffee   Hot Rolls

Lemon Cloud Dessert

Jackies' Plantation Pralines

69

So on to February and Papa first. The ambrosia recipe has been given on page 16, but do cut it in half for a first course for six persons.

All good Creole dishes seem to begin with a richly browned roux. The Gumbo is no exception

Seafood Gumbo

the roux: In a heavy iron pot melt 3 Tablespoons oil and add 3 Tablespoons flour.

Cook and stir with a wooden spoon over medium heat until brown. Do not allow to smoke.

Add:

3 large onions, chopped
1½ lbs okra (fresh okra that has been washed, stemmed and sliced very thin).
2 Tablespoons cooking oil
1 Tablespoon vinegar

Cook over medium heat a few minutes. Reduce the heat a little. Salt and pepper to taste. Cook, covered, until okra is almost tender. Stir only once or twice.

72 Add:

4 cups chicken broth
3 large ripe tomatoes, peeled and chopped
3 Tablespoons tomato paste
3 Tablespoons dry beef bouillon

Cook 20 minutes more.

At this point the mixture may be frozen if desired. The day you plan to serve the gumbo, remove from the freezer early in the day. About an hour before dinner (or before your guests arrive) add 1½ lbs. of shrimp, lobster and/or crab and cook for 30 minutes over low heat. A combination of all three seafoods makes a delicious gumbo. Serve with boiled or instant rice. Serves six - generously. Use large individual soup plates.

Papa's Salad

1 large head Boston lettuce
1 head Iceberg lettuce
1 1 lb. size head Romaine lettuce
6 radishes, sliced thin
3 green onions, chopped
3 stalks of celery, cut coarsely
1 carrot, sliced thin
1 cup cooked green beans, chilled
1 small jar artichoke hearts
1 avacado, diced
½ a red pepper, cut in thin strips

Wash and drain greens, break into bite size pieces in a very large salad bowl. Refrigerate.

Just before serving, toss everything lightly with 1 cup of your favorite oil and vinegar dressing. Serve in individual salad bowls - serves 8 generously.

With the gumbo and this salad you will need only bread and butter. Hot french bread or rolls will do nicely. A light dessert.

Lemon Cloud

1 small package lemon gelatin
1 cup boiling water
1/2 pint whipping cream
1 cup sugar
2 lemons, juice and grated rind
1/4 cup lemonade concentrate
1 1/2 cups vanilla wafer or graham cracker crumbs

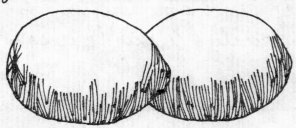

Dissolve the gelatin in the boiling water and chill until partially set. Whip the cream — very stiff—and add the sugar, lemon juice and rind, and the concentrate. Fold with gelatin.

Pour this into a 9"x 13"x 2" glass pan that has been buttered and lined with the cookie or cracker crumbs. Reserve a few crumbs for the top — sprinkle over lightly and refrigerate for several hours. Cut into squares, serve with extra dollop of cream or plain. Serves 12 to 15.

Jackie's Pralines

2 cups sugar
1 teaspoon baking soda
1 cup buttermilk

3 Tablespoons butter
1 teaspoon vanilla
2 cups pecan halves

78

Prepare a large sheet of waxed paper by buttering it generously. Put aside on a heat-proof surface.

In a large kettle cook the sugar, baking soda and buttermilk. Stirring constantly with a large wooden spoon, cook for 5 minutes after it begins to boil or to 210° if you have a candy thermometer. Add butter, a pinch of salt, vanilla, and pecans. Cook and stir until soft ball stage or 230°. Remove from heat. Cool slightly. Beat until creamy. When it just begins to look dull, start dropping teaspoons of the candy onto the buttered waxed paper. Work very fast. If you can get help do so because speed in dropping the mounds onto the paper is essential. This is an old Mississippi recipe - very rich and delicious. I am grateful to Jackie and her family for sharing this old favorite with us. These are best the day they are made.

Mothers' Birthday
February 12th

Tomato juice cocktail
Standing Prime Rib Roast
Yorkshire Pudding
Brown Roasted Potatoes
Honey glazed carrots julienne
Bundt Cake – thin orange icing
or Lincoln Log
Coffee

Mother and Lincoln shared the same day if not the same year.

Standing Rib Roast

A 3 or 4 rib roast will usually serve 5 or 6 persons. This will depend on the roast (bone, fat and other waste). Wipe the meat and place in a shallow baking or roasting pan. Place the roast in a preheated oven set at 475°. Check roast frequently. When it is brown take the pan from the oven and add small peeled potatoes to the pan. Salt and pepper the roast. Reduce the oven heat to 325°, insert a meat thermometer in the roast and continue to cook. While the potatoes cook turn them a few times so they brown evenly.

83

Figure on 2 small potatoes per person plus 2 or 3 extra for insurance. Your meat thermometer will tell you when the roast is done to your liking — we like ours rare so I remove it to a hot platter at 135°.

Put the pan roasted potatoes in a hot, covered dish and keep warm.

Remove 6 Tablespoons of the pan drippings to a loaf pan and return it to the oven which is once more set at 425°. Have the pudding ready.

84

Mother's Yorkshire Pudding

1/4 cup flour
1/4 teaspoon salt
3/4 cup milk

3 large eggs
the 6 Tablespoons drippings

Mix the flour and salt, gradually add the milk. Separate the eggs. Beat the yolks and add to the flour mixture. Beat the whites very stiff. Fold whites gently into flour mixture.

Pull out the oven rack with the pan of hot drippings on it. Leave the pan on the rack and quickly turn the pudding mixture into the hot fat. Close the oven quickly and bake at 425° for 15 minutes; reduce the heat to 350° and bake another 10 minutes. By the time the pudding is finished everything else should be ready for serving.

Pan Gravy

If there are more than 4 Tablespoons of fat left in the roasting pan, pour off the excess. Heat the 4 Tablespoons of fat with 4 Tablespoons flour. Stir continuously and brown about 5 minutes. Add 2½ cups of any good beef stock or add 2 teaspoons instant bouillon to 2½ cups water. Scrape down the sides of the pan and continue cooking on low heat for about 10 minutes. Serve in a hot gravy boat. During this time the carrots can be taking on a honey glaze.

Honey Glazed Carrots

The day before your party, cook enough whole, peeled carrots for each guest to have 1 large or 2 small ones . Cook these in enough water to cover them (just barely) and add 1/4 cup sugar. It will take about 20 minutes. When the carrots are quite tender remove from the heat and cool to room temperature. Cut into Julienne strips, put them in a jar, and cover with enough of the cooking liquid to fill the jar, seal and refrigerate. For six persons: melt one stick of butter in a large saucepan (this is on the day of your party), add

3/4 cup honey and a little grated orange rind.
Remove the cooked carrots from the refrigerator.
Drain and add to the honey glaze. Turn heat to
low and cook for 15 or 20 minutes. Shake a few
times and check to see that the carrots do not stick
or burn. Serve in a hot vegetable dish.

Simple Bundt Cake

1 box Lemon Cake mix (I do use short cuts)
1 package instant lemon pudding

3/4 cup milk   4 large eggs
3/4 cup oil   grated rind of ½ a lemon

    Beat all together in an electric mixer for about 20 minutes at medium speed.

    Bake in greased and floured Bundt cake pan at 350° for about 45 minutes. Test with a tooth pick for doneness. It will come out clean if cake is done. Cool for 5 minutes in pan. Turn out onto a cake plate and drizzle with the icing.

Orange Icing

2 Tablespoons butter
3 Tablespoons orange juice
2 cups confectioners' sugar, sifted

Melt the butter, add the juice and the sugar. Beat well. When it is quite creamy, drizzle over the cake — fill the center hole, too. Serves 10 generously.

With the Bundt Cake just serve plenty of coffee. And there you have it.

Lincoln Log

4 eggs
3/4 cup sugar
1 teaspoon baking powder
1/4 teaspoon salt

1/2 cup flour
6 Tablespoons cocoa
1 teaspoon vanilla

Make a chocolate (jelly type) roll: Beat the whole eggs over hot water until fluffy. Add the sugar, baking powder, and salt, a little at a time, beating well all the while. Sift the flour and cocoa together. Fold into the eggs and add the vanilla. Pour onto a cookie tin with a 1" lip all around that has been greased, lined with waxed paper and greased again. Bake at 400° for 15 minutes. Turn out quickly onto a pastry cloth lightly covered with powdered sugar.

Remove the waxed paper quickly, cut away any crisp or too-brown edges. Roll up cake and towel together. When cool, or at serving time, unroll and fill with: your favorite cream or this:

Cream Filling

2 cups of heavy cream   ½ cup of sugar
¼ teaspoon cream of tartar   1 teaspoon vanilla

     Whip the cream very stiff with the cream of tartar. As soft peaks form, gradually add the sugar and the vanilla. Beat until stiff and spread on the chocolate roll. Roll up again and wrap with waxed paper until ready to slice

     Melt a bar of German chocolate with ½ cup heavy cream. Cook over low heat 'til smooth and thick. Cool slightly and ice the roll.

Strawberry Cheesecake

3   8 oz packages cream cheese
6 egg whites
2 teaspoons vanilla
1 1/8 cup of sugar

Topping:
1 cup sour cream
1/3 cup sugar
1 teaspoon vanilla

9*

Prepare a 9" spring form pan by buttering
it well and dusting it with 1 cup of toast
(Zwiebach) crumbs.

Have the cream cheese at room temperature. Beat thoroughly. Beat egg whites stiff and - gradually add the 1⅛ cups sugar and 2 teaspoons vanilla. Add the stiffly beaten mixture gently to the cream cheese and pour into the pan. Bake for 30 minutes at 350°. Remove from oven and spread quickly with the sour cream mixed with ⅓ cup sugar and 1 teaspoon vanilla. Bake at 425° for 12 minutes more. Remove to rack and cool thoroughly in the pan. Place the cake on a serving plate and top with this.

Strawberry Topping

1 large package frozen strawberries, thawed
3/4 cup sugar mixed with 2 Tablespoons cornstarch
juice of 1/2 lemon
dash of salt
1 Tablespoon sweet butter

96

     Cook all together over medium heat until thick and chear, stirring continuously. This will take about 10 minutes, perhaps a little longer.
     Cool, and top the cheesecake, drizzling some over the sides. Decorate with mint leaves or a

few fresh berries if they happen to be in season.
Serves 12 - can be stretched to 16. So much for
Valentine's.

So 'tis on to March and St. Patrick's Day and sure and you don't have to be Irish to like the way we celebrate the day!

Whether we had guests or not we always had the same menu.

St. Patrick's Menu

Boiled Corned Beef with Vegetables
(carrots, onions and potatoes)
Shredded Cabbage and butter
Horseradish Sauce
Cornbread   Soft butter
Green tomato relish or
chow - chow
Lime Chiffon Pie (Bernies')
Coffee

100

Corned Beef

1 stalk of celery
1 onion
1 carrot
2 small potatoes, 2 small carrots, 1 onion per
     person to be served
3 Tablespoons flour
2 Tablespoons horseradish

Wash a 4 or 5 pound corned beef brisket, cover with water and bring to a boil in a large pan. If the boiling water is too salty, pour off and cover the meat again with fresh water, and again bring to a boil. Reduce the heat, add the single onion, carrot and stalk of celery, cover, and cook about 4 hours or 'til fork-tender. Remove meat and seasoning vegetables; pour off and reserve 2½ cups of broth. Check the saltiness of the broth and add salt if needed. Season with freshly ground black pepper and add the rest of the vegetables.

Cover and cook until tender – about ½ hour for the onions and carrots, a little less for the potatoes. Remove and keep warm.

To make the sauce, blend the flour with cold water to a smooth paste, add to broth remaining in pan, add the horseradish and boil over very low heat until thick. Cover and keep warm. Just before serving the sauce add 3 sprigs of parsley, minced.

Green Cabbage

      With the 2 cups of reserved broth, boiling on low heat, prepare the cabbage and add to the pot. Get green cabbage if you can, wash and drain it, then shred it as you do for cole slaw. Turn the heat to high and when the cabbage begins to boil, stir it well and cover it with a tight-fitting lid. Reduce the heat somewhat, but continue to boil for 5 minutes. Pour off the broth and add ¼ cup butter. Cover and keep warm or serve immediately.

Make the cornbread given in the Christmas menu or buy heat - and - serve muffins. Serve with sweet butter.

This is a hearty dinner and the sauce adds the zest it needs, so pass the sauceboat often. Serve the corned beef (sliced) on a large platter with the carrots, onions and potatoes. Garnish with a few sprigs of parsley. Serve the cabbage in a covered dish.

105

Follow this with a sweet, green dessert -
something light, such as:

Bernies' Lime Pie

106

¼ cup water
½ cup lime juice
1 envelope gelatin
1 cup sugar

¼ teaspoon salt
4 large eggs - separated
grated rind of 2 limes
green food coloring

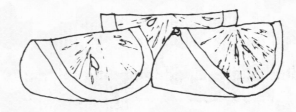

Mix the lime juice and water. Sprinkle the gelatin over the top. Wait 5 minutes, then mix. Add ½ cup sugar, the salt and the beaten egg yolks. Beat. Cook over low heat or boiling water until the mixture coats the spoon and is quite thick and smooth. It will require stirring during this cooking. Add the rind.

Beat the egg whites to soft peaks, add the ½ cup sugar gradually and beat very stiff. Fold into the egg filling and add the coloring. Pour into a baked 9" pie shell or use a 9" graham cracker crumb shell. You can find both in the frozen food section of your market or make your own. Refrigerate overnight.

Just before you serve it, frost the entire pie with whipped cream. One pint of heavy cream whipped with ¼ cup sugar and a little lemon juice will frost the pie nicely. This seems the last of winter. Soon there will be fresh asparagus, strawberries and rhubarb - ah spring!

Easter Morning Brunch

Orange juice   Broiled grapefruit
Eggs a la' goldenrod
    Pork Sausage / Bacon
Blueberry muffins   coffee
    Hot Coffeecake

110

Have ½ grapefruit for each guest. Broil with 1 Tablespoon brown sugar on each half at the last minute before the meal. About 5 minutes should do it - Watch them!

Put the bacon on a broiler rack and broil

it, along with the brown and serve sausage, in the oven. Set the oven at 425° and allow 20 minutes or a little longer depending on the thickness of the bacon. For, the sausage, check the package for directions on timing.

Sauce for the eggs (goldenrod) can be made a day or two ahead and refrigerated. See next page: (to serve 8 persons):

Goldenrod Sauce

6 Tablespoons margarine
8 Tablespoons flour
2 cups milk

½ teaspoon salt
dash of white pepper
1 cup light cream

112   Melt the margarine - stir well, add the flour, cook and slowly add milk, salt, and the white pepper. Cook until thick. Refrigerate.

      The day it is to be served, heat 1 cup light cream and gradually beat into the cream sauce prepared earlier, stir continuously over low heat.

Separate egg yolks from the whites of 1 dozen hard-boiled eggs. Slice the whites into the cream sauce, cover and keep warm. Sieve the egg yolks and put these in an attractive serving dish.

The creamed whites may be served at the table from your chafing dish. Have plenty of toast points on which to serve the sauce and top this with the sieved egg yolks. Pass the meat platter with the bacon and sausage.

Easter Sunday Dinner

Baked Ham   Spiced Fruit
Fresh buttered Asparagus
Wilted Leaf Lettuce Salad
Sweet red pepper relish
Hot Rolls or Hot Cross Buns
White Chocolate Easter Cake
Coffee

114

Bake the ham on Saturday. Just heat and serve on Sunday.

Spiced Fruit

peach halves — 1 per person
pear halves — 1 per person
1½ cups mixed fruit juices
½ cup Sauterne
1 Tablespoon curry powder
2 Tablespoons arrowroot or cornstarch
½ cup brown sugar
maraschino cherries

115

Use canned halves of peaches, and pears. For 8 persons bring the juices and wine to a boil over medium heat. Mix the curry powder and the arrowroot or cornstarch with enough water to make a thin paste. Stir into juice and add the brown sugar and taste for salt. Cook until slightly thickened.

Arrange fruit in baking dish, add the cherries for color. Pour sauce over fruit and bake at 350° for 30 minutes. Sauce dishes for serving this, please.

Asparagus

If you have traditional foods for this day by all means include these in your work schedule.

Since most of the menu is oven fare this is an easy dinner. I hope you have an asparagus cooker or steamer. If not then: tie the fresh asparagus with kitchen string and set the bundles with the "tips" up. Cook in a deep saucepan in boiling salted water with another pan inverted over the top, or if a lid will fit use that. Cook for about 15 minutes - depending on the size and age of the vegetable. Drain and serve with butter on a vegetable platter.

Wilted Lettuce

1½ lbs leaf lettuce (early spring type)
3 tender green onions, chopped–green tops, too

Make a Vinegar Sauce:

118

8 slices bacon cut into ¼ th's
½ cup vinegar
¼ cup sugar
¼ cup water
salt and pepper

Fry the bacon in a heavy fry pan until crisp. Remove from pan and drain on paper towel. Add the remaining ingredients to the bacon fat. Boil up for about 5 minutes. Set aside.

Place greens (torn into bite size pieces) in a large salad bowl, add the green onion and bacon. Salt and pepper and boil up the sauce once more. Pour over greens, toss quickly and serve.

White Chocolate Easter Cake

¼ lb white chocolate, melted
1 cup butter
2 cups sugar
5 eggs
1 cup buttermilk
2½ cups flour
⅓ teaspoon salt
1 teaspoon vanilla
1 teaspoon baking powder
1 cup moist coconut
1 cup chopped nuts (walnuts or pecans)

120

Melt the chocolate, cool. Cream the butter and sugar. Add the chocolate. Add the eggs one at a time, beating well after each. Sift the remaining dry ingredients; add these alternately with the buttermilk [to the cream batter] Fold in vanilla, coconut and nuts. Pour into greased and floured 9" cake pans. Bake at 350° for about 1 hour. Invert on wire racks to cool.

121

Frosting

1 cup sugar
1/3 cup water
1/3 cup light corn syrup

2 (large) egg whites
1 teaspoon vanilla
cream of tartar

Cook the sugar, water and corn syrup, covered, 123
for 5 minutes. Remove cover and cook until the
syrup spins a thread. Meanwhile beat the whites
with 1/3 teaspoon cream of tartar until stiff.
Continue to beat and gradually add the hot
syrup - in a very thin stream at first. Add the
vanilla and continue to beat until the frosting

holds its shape.

Frost the layers and decorate with little colored eggs and a few candied wintergreen leaves or fresh mint leaves if you have them. Candied violets are lovely if you are not "thinking Easter".

<u>Easter Supper</u>

Norwegian Pancakes Almdale
with Strawberries - sour cream
Smokies   Hot Coffee

Norwegian Pancakes Almdale

9 eggs
1 cup milk

½ teaspoon salt
½ cup flour, sifted

Beat with a large wooden spoon, one egg at a time until you have added all nine, beating well after each egg. Add the milk and salt. Beat. Sift 2 Tablespoons of flour at a time over the egg mixture until it is gone. The batter should be very smooth. If it is _not_ satin smooth I have a trick for you to which I'm sure no self-respecting Almdale would

125

stoop. I work the batter through a sieve. Use the wooden spoon for this also (and I hope you know the difference between a sieve and a colander!). Refrigerate overnight if you wish. The day you use it, beat again to blend. Heat 2 cast iron fry pans or 2 heavy fry pans 10" in diameter. Oil well with Mazola or Wesson oil. Pour 2 Tablespoons batter, or enough to cover the bottom of the pan when you tilt it, and swirl the batter around (as for crepés). Cook over medium heat for about 2 minutes. Turn carefully with a wide spatula.

Cook on the other side until lightly brown-about 3 minutes. Remove from pan and very quickly roll up and put on hot platter in keep-warm oven. Continue to make pancakes until all the batter is cooked.

I like to serve warm plates with the pancakes like this - quickly unroll and fill with strawberry sauce and a tablespoon of sour cream. Roll up again and put a pat or two of soft sweet butter on top.

Serve brown-and-serve smoky sausages
with this.

Count on the men to eat three or four and
the ladies less. For our four this recipe is just
128 enough, so try it on your family and see what
quantity you'll need.

The sausages and the pancakes along
with the serving plates could be in the keep-warm
oven.

Strawberry Filling

1 pint box of fresh strawberries
1 10 ounce jar strawberry preserves
2 Tablespoons butter
½ cup water

129

    Wash and hull the strawberries, drain. Bring the ½ cup water to a rolling boil in a saucepan over high heat. Add the jar of strawberry preserves. Cook and stir until well blended - 2 or 3 minutes.
    Reduce the heat to medium and add the

fresh berries and the butter. Cook 5 or 6 minutes. The strawberries should be tender but still quite whole. Cook a little longer if necessary. Serve the extra sauce another time if there is any left. It is also very good on vanilla ice cream.

130

Serve plenty of hot coffee with this. One more word about the filling - be sure the sour cream is left at room temperature for several hours - otherwise it cools the pancakes too much!

Grandma G. had her turn in September but now that I try to recall - we didn't always have the same menu. Her most frequent choice was Leg O' Lamb, but many times she chose such unexpected favorites as Liver with Onions, which she loved.

132

Grandma Groceman's September Birthday Menu

Fruit Cup

Leg O' Lamb   Mint Jelly

Parsley Potatoes

Tiny Peas and Onions, Creamed

Wilted Spinach Salad

Coffee

Vienna Almond Torte (Cake)

A salute to Grandma here, for she was a marvelous cook.

Fruit Cup for Autumn

2 apples, finely chopped
1 pound of grapes cut in half and seeded (if you
   can't get Thompson seedless)
1/4 cup chopped pecans
134 1/4 cup sugar

     Mix apple, grapes, and sugar. Refrigerate.
Serve a small amount in your stemmed glass
sherbets and sprinkle a chopped pecan on top.

Spring seems more the time for lamb but here it is for a September dinner

Baked Leg O' Lamb

5 or 6 pound leg of lamb
2 garlic cloves, - sliced
salt and pepper

Bake in a shallow pan on a little meat rack. Wipe the lamb and make little slits in the

skin with a sharp knife. Insert the garlic slices in the slits.

Set the oven at 325°. When the lamb has browned nicely, add water to the pan and salt and pepper the roast well. Return to the oven and continue to bake until the thermometer reads 182° for a well-done roast.

Parsley Potatoes

Parboil 2 small, red potatoes per serving, 12 potatoes for 6 people. Cut a circle of the red skin from around the center of each potato.

Now melt 4 Tablespoons butter in a baking dish. Add 2 Tablespoons finely chopped parsley and the little potatoes. Set aside. The last half hour before dinner, pop these in the oven at 350°.

137

Very early in the day wash and check over the spinach. Drain it well and refrigerate it.

Wilted Spinach

½ lb bacon
3/4 cup vinegar
¼ cup water
2/3 cup sugar

2 eggs, hard-boiled
4 green onions, chopped
spinach

Fry the bacon in a heavy pan and drain.

Pour off the fat, measure 1/3 cup and return it to the pan. Add vinegar, water, and sugar. Bring to a boil over high heat; reduce the heat and cook down about 10 minutes. Set aside.

Crumble the bacon. At serving time put the uncooked spinach in a very large salad bowl, sprinkle the top with the onions; add the eggs, chopped fine; the crumbled bacon; salt and pepper to taste - be generous with this.

Bring the dressing to a boil again, pour over the salad and serve it quickly.

139

Tiny Peas and Onions, Creamed

Melt 2 Tablespoons butter and add 2 Tablespoons flour. Cook a few seconds, then add 1 cup rich milk or light cream. Cook and stir until thick and smooth, remove from heat, add salt and pepper to taste. Cover and set aside.

Just at serving time cook frozen tiny peas and little onions (separately) according to package directions.

Drain the vegetables. Heat the cream sauce and add 1 Tablespoon Dry Sherry. Add the peas and onions.

Vienna Almond Torte

1 cup crumbs made of Zwieback toast
1 cup ground almonds
12 eggs, separated
2 cups sugar
½ teaspoon cinnamon
grated rind of ½ lemon and ½ orange

    Roll the Zwieback toast into very fine crumbs. Set aside.
    Beat egg yolks and sugar for 20 minutes in the electric mixer. Add the nuts, cinnamon,

and grated rind. Add the stiffly beaten egg whites - fold gently. Last, add the toast crumbs. Bake in 4 greased 9" cake pans lined with waxed

143

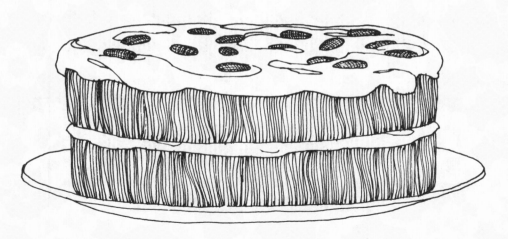

paper and greased again. Bake at 325° for about 1 hour or until it springs back when you lightly touch the top with your finger. Cool a minute, then invert on racks and quickly remove the paper. Cool thoroughly and put together with sweetened whipped cream. Unless you are having a very large party, put only two layers together and put the other two in the freezer for a later date. Decorate the top with the sweetened whipped cream when ready to serve and add a few toasted almonds as a finishing touch.

With the crisp October days Brother Bob looked
forward to his favorite season and his Birthday

Bob's Birthday Menu

146

Soft Apple Cider - Edam Wedge
Swiss Steak - Gravy
Mashed Potatoes
Cauliflower   Green Beans
Hot Bread - Butter - Lettuce Wedge
Banana Cake   Coffee

Swiss Steak

Buy a top round steak 1" to 1¼" thick (about 2
    pounds)
1 cup flour
¼ cup green pepper, chopped
½ cup chopped onion
½ cup celery
1 bouillon cube
1 cup tomato juice
4 Tablespoons oil
salt and pepper

147

With the side of a heavy luncheon plate pound the steak on both sides a few times. Salt and pepper the meat and pound in as much of the 1 cup of flour as the meat will absorb. Do both sides.

Heat the oil in a Dutch Oven. With the heat on high, add the steak. Brown quickly on both sides. Add the onion and brown it lightly. Add the green pepper, chopped celery, bouillon, and tomato juice. Cover tightly, reduce the heat to simmer and cook for 2 hours or until fork —

tender. After the first half hour, check the moisture in the pot - add more tomato juice if needed or add water if you like.

Remove the meat to a platter and cook the sauce down a bit without the lid. If the sauce is thick you will not need to cook it down (this depends on your meat and will vary greatly). Serve the sauce in a separate boat or, if there is a small quantity, pour it over the meat.

With this serve your fluffiest mashed potatoes, green beans, and cauliflower.

Banana Cake   -   Serves 12

1 cup sugar
3 tablespoons shortening
1/4 cup corn oil
2 eggs
150   1 1/2 cups flour
1 teaspoon baking soda
1/4 teaspoon salt
3/4 cup pecans
1/3 cup raisins
1/2 teaspoon cinnamon   1/4 teaspoon cloves
3 mashed bananas, (ripe ones, please)

Cream oil, shortening, and sugar. Add eggs. Beat thoroughly and add the bananas.

Sift dry ingredients, add nuts and raisins. Fold into creamed batter.

Bake in two greased and floured 9" cake pans at 350° for 30 minutes or until done. Invert on wire racks and cool. Ice when completely cool.

Icing

½ cup butter
1 cup sugar
½ cup Eagle Brand Milk
1 teaspoon vanilla
152 dash of salt
pecans

   Mix butter, sugar, salt, and milk. Let stand
for at least an hour. Cook, stirring constantly,
to the soft ball stage or 232°. Remove from heat.
Cool to lukewarm. Beat until it is spreading

consistency.

　　Place a layer on a cake plate, spread with a small amount of the icing. Slice a firm banana over the icing and place the second layer over the first. Ice the sides and top with remaining icing. Sprinkle with about ½ cup pecan halves.

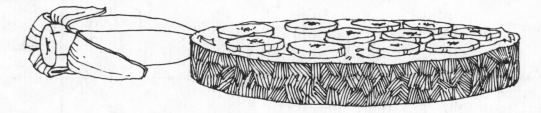

Fred's Birthday

Southern Fried Chicken
Mashed Potatoes   Cream Gravy
Tiny buttered Peas   Tossed Salad
Hot Biscuits   with   Honey Butter
              Coffee
Chocolate Pie   Cake

155

Southern Fried Chicken

5 whole chicken legs cut into "long legs" and
    "short legs" or thighs
2 chicken breasts
salt, pepper, flour
156 Mazola or Wesson oil

Heat a Dutch oven with enough oil to almost
cover the chicken. Start with about an inch and when
you add the chicken (the first piece) add more oil
and let it get really hot before adding the rest of
the chicken.

Wipe the chicken pieces; salt, pepper, and flour them well. I like to cut a wish bone and then cut the breast into two pieces. This makes six pieces of breast from 2 whole ones.

Fry in hot fat until golden on one side, turn and brown the other side. Do not crowd. One Dutch oven will not cook sixteen pieces at once. When done, drain on paper towels and keep the chicken in a warm oven. Pour off most of the oil left in the pan. You will need about 4 Tablespoons of oil and 4 Tablespoons flour for 2 cups of gravy. Cook the flour-oil mixture briefly and add 2 cups of milk and ½ cup of cream. Cook and stir until the gravy thickens. Taste and adjust the seasoning. This gravy should not be too salty. Cover until ready to serve. If it thickens too much during the keep-warm period just add a little milk or cream.

158

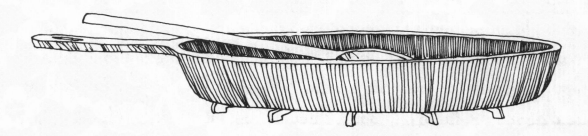

Use tiny frozen peas and cook according to the package directions.

One package will serve three persons so prepare as many packages as you will need. Just add butter and you have a lovely green vegetable. 159

Use your favorite tossed salad recipe and oil and vinegar dressing.

Whip butter with enough honey to taste. The honey butter should be fluffy but not syrupy. Pile it into a pretty dish and put it in the refrigerator until an hour before dinner.

If you really want the best biscuits in the whole world, make these.

Sourmilk Biscuits

Sift together:

2½ cups flour	1 teaspoon salt
4 teaspoons baking powder	½ teaspoon baking soda

Cut ½ cup shortening into the dry ingredients

(as you would for a pie crust). When the mixture resembles cornmeal add 1¼ cups buttermilk or sour milk. Mix.

Turn out onto a well-floured cloth or board. Knead lightly. Pat or roll out about ½" thick.

Meanwhile heat 3 Tablespoons oil in a bread pan. When the oil is very hot cut the biscuits with a round cutter the size you like best (I prefer the smaller cutter). Dip the biscuits in the hot fat, turn over and arrange in the pan. By the time all of the biscuits have been cut and arranged all the oil should be used.

  If you are preparing these for a party you can do this much and then refrigerate them. 30 minutes before you wish to serve take them out of the refrigerator and set in a warm place. Bake 15 minutes later in a 450° oven for 12 minutes. They should be a golden brown. Rush to the table. Serve with honey butter.

Fred's Favorite Chocolate Pie

1½ cups flour
½ teaspoon salt
5 Tablespoons margarine
3 Tablespoons shortening

5 Tablespoons ice water
2 Tablespoons vegetable oil

164

   Make a 10" pie crust like this: Sift flour and salt together in a large mixing bowl. Cut into this the margarine and shortening. When it is blended to the "small crumbs" stage add the ice water and oil. Mix lightly with a fork until it holds together. Make a ball and lay it on a floured pastry cloth. Allow to "rest" a few minutes. Sprinkle with flour and roll out with a well-floured rolling-pin 1" larger than your pie pan.

Fit the pastry carefully into the pan. Flute the edges, pressing the pastry against the sides. Prick the bottom and sides in several places. Bake at 475° for 8 to 10 minutes. Should the pastry puff up in spite of all you've done, quickly open the oven and prick the spot with a fork. When the shell is a nice light brown remove it to a rack.

When the crust is quite cool fill it with Aunt Gladys' Chocolate meringue filling.

Chocolate Meringue Filling

1½ cups sugar
3 squares unsweetened chocolate
½ teaspoon salt
3 Tablespoons cornstarch
1 Tablespoon flour
3 cups milk

¼ cup cream
2 Tablespoons butter
2 teaspoons vanilla
½ cup sugar
5 large eggs, separated
¼ teaspoon of cream of tartar

167

    Mix 1½ cups sugar, salt, flour, and cornstarch in saucepan. Gradually add the milk and cream. Add the chocolate cut into shavings. Cook and stir over medium heat until mixture thickens. Boil a

few seconds more and remove from heat. Beat
the egg yolks well and add a little of the hot
mixture to them - beating very fast.

Gradually add more of the hot mixture to
168 the eggs. Now pour the yolks into the remaining
chocolate cream in the pan. Return to heat and
cook for 2 or 3 minutes. Remove from the heat—
add the butter and vanilla - blend. Cool slightly
before pouring into the cooled pie shell.

The Meringue

Beat the 5 egg whites until foamy with the cream of tartar. Add a dash of salt and the ½ cup sugar - adding it only two tablespoons at a time. Beat until stiff peaks form. Cover the chocolate filling, being very careful to seal the meringue to the crust. Bake at 400° for 10 to 12 minutes or until delicately brown. Cool at room temperature away from drafts. This is rich and should serve 6 to 8 persons.

169

Patti's Birthday

Rump Roast   Brown Gravy
Mashed Potatoes
Kentucky Wonder Green Beans
Buttered Corn
Grated Carrot Salad   Hot Rolls
Macadamia Nut Birthday Cake
Mints   Coffee

170

These are only a few of our family favorites. Change the menus around anyway you like, but remember to exchange a like item for like item (ie. a green vegetable should only be changed to another green unless you are also changing the salad). Look at the <u>whole</u> and be sure that it pleases.

Rump roast has been neglected as an oven roast. It really is tender and delicious this way.

Rump Roast

Buy a 5 or 6 pound roast. Not rolled, nicely marbled, but without those gristly seams.

Wipe the meat and place on a little rack in a shallow pan. Roast at 325° until well done. After the meat browns, remove it from the oven, salt and pepper it and add enough water to cover the bottom of the pan. Continue to roast, adding more water to the pan as needed. A well-done 6 pound roast will take about 3 hours. The meat thermometer should read 170°. Remove the meat to a platter and keep warm.

172

Gravy

To the beautifully browned drippings in the pan add enough beef stock to make about 3 cups. Boil up and add 5 Tablespoons flour mixed with cold water to make a thin paste. Stir vigorously while adding the flour. Bring to a boil, reduce the heat and simmer a few minutes. Serve very hot in a gravy boat.

Prepare your own mashed potatoes but do have plenty. With this kind of gravy everyone will eat seconds!

Grandmother always canned Kentucky Wonder green beans. We seemed to end up with a few jars just for Patti.

Now this special variety of bean is grown even in New Jersey. If you are not able to get the true Kentucky Wonders use the frozen green beans.

If you can get fresh corn, do so. At serving time have the corn ready for the pan. Boil up a large kettle of water with 1/4 cup sugar. Add the ears of corn and when the water returns to a boil cook the corn 5 minutes and take it out of the water.

Serve with plenty of butter and have the salt and pepper mill handy. I have the corn for Patti, but for guests I'd skip the corn and have just the green beans. If you prefer the corn over the beans then have a green salad.

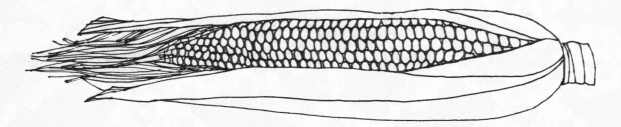

Carrot Salad

6 large carrots, medium grated
½ cup coconut flakes
½ cup mayonnaise
1 Tablespoon sugar
176 sour cream to bind

Put the carrots, coconut and mayonnaise into a large bowl and toss lightly (this amount is for 6 servings). Add the sugar and enough sour cream to bind the carrots together. Chill for several hours. Serve on greens.

Macadamia Nut Cake

For this you will need a large orange or lemon chiffon cake. Bake one day or two ahead or buy one at the market.

1 pint heavy cream
1/4 teaspoon cream of tartar
1/2 cup sugar
1 teaspoon vanilla
1 can pineapple pie filling
1/2 cup toasted coconut flakes

Whip the cream with the cream of tartar, sugar, and vanilla. This should be very stiff.

Use the pineapple pie filling and the coconut flakes between the layers. Dividing the pie filling and coconut equally, spread ½ over the bottom layer, add a small amount of the whipped cream. Put the second layer on top and use the other half of the can of pie filling on it, sprinkle the remaining half of toasted coconut over the filling, add a small amount of the whipped cream and top with the third cake layer.

Frost the whole cake with the remaining whipped cream. If there is enough cream, fill the center hole, also.

Chop 4 ounces macadamia nuts fine and sprinkle the cake with these.

Refrigerate for 2 hours. Serves 10.

Index